IT DEMANDS
A WILDNESS OF ME

An Anthology

Poets—

Lee Darling
Laura LeHew
Catherine McGuire
Sharon Lask Munson
Janice D. Rubin
Renate Tilson
Harriot West

Editor—

Laura LeHew

First U.S. edition 2017

Editors/Publisher: Laura LeHew

Proofreaders: Keli Osborn
    Quinton Hallett
    Roy R. Seitz

Cover: "The Riveter"
    © Laura LeHew, 2017

This single extraordinary rose symbolizes the underlying theme of this anthology: unforgettable. LeHew shot this photo at the Owen Rose Garden in Eugene, Oregon in the spring of 2017 at 8:15 in the morning. You can find her there most Tuesdays and Wednesdays.

Copyright © 2017   Uttered Chaos

Uttered Chaos
PO Box 50638
Eugene, OR 97405
www.utteredchaos.org

ISBN: 978-0-9889366-8-3

A NOTE OF GRATITUDE:

Thanks to the Lane Literary Guild (LLG) for its generous contribution to Uttered Chaos of $225. We extend our gratitude for their support of a literary work for the Rhetorical Devices critique group through their grant-making activity.

This grant was used to assist us in production of this anthology and includes works from current Lane Literary Guild/Rhetorical Devices members Lee Darling, Laura LeHew, Catherine McGuire, Sharon Lask Munson, Janice D. Rubin, Renate Tilson and Harriot West.

Grant funding is important to our literary organization and our community. This anthology showcases both the individual members and the cohesiveness of the group. We hope it will also serve as continuing outreach to the poetry community at large.

For more information on the LLG:

laneliteraryguild.org

Laura LeHew

and her many hats—
Uttered Chaos Editor
Lane Literary Guild Steering Committee
Rhetorical Devices Facilitator

CONTENTS

INTRODUCTION

Henry Alley. President, Lane Literary Guild, 1986, 2017

My first reading for the Lane Literary Guild came on April 29, 1985. It was at Maude Kerns Art Gallery, close to the university, with spring light coming into the large hall. As Howard Robertson's "The Lane Literary Guild: A Brief History," will tell you, the Guild had been going about a year, and was finding its way, having originated from an idea that had visited Ingrid Wendt in 1983. The idea was realized through the work of many, including Bill Sweet, my neighbor and a poet, Steven White, poet and translator, and poet Ingrid herself. As for a number of writers who joined the Guild in its early days, being a part of the reading series served as a turning point in building my relationship to the outside world. The Guild, over the years, was extremely successful in its mission of connecting an enormous amount of local talent to a wide audience.

In my estimation, the poems in this anthology are a part of a signature aspect of the Guild—finding shape and self-discovery in the natural world and sharing it with a group of like-minded and aesthetically oriented Lane County people. The message frequently is—and has been in the many readings which I have attended in the thirty-plus years to follow—that we do not have to look far to perceive the beautiful, but we need to have the help of the neighboring poet's or the writer's eye for full disclosure. Let us affirm the unusual in the usual, many of these poets seem to say. The consistency of this message, even among poets as diverse as those represented here, should not be surprising, given the amount of beauty Lane County residents live with on a daily basis.

Unlike my reading on April 29, 1985, my actual first involvement with the Guild, presumably in 1984, close to when it started, is not recorded. However, I do remember some of the circumstances. We were all having a picnic down close to the Willamette River, and we discussed how we were going to have William Stafford—who seems like something of a patron saint of poetry here in Oregon—come to Eugene as one of our readers. I would like to say as an inaugural reader. Bill Sweet was personal friends with him, and so we all put our heads together as to how he would visit and how we would promote his reading. This event shows another hallmark of the Guild—we all get behind the poet or the writer, whether he or she is famous or not.

Laura LeHew, the editor of this anthology, stands in the full spirit of this Lane Literary Guild history. She promotes the known and the not-so-well-known and puts "image" and turn of phrase first. It is a pleasure to see her mission be another manifestation of our vision and carry forward a tradition that goes back more than thirty years.

FROM THE OTHER SIDE
An encounter at the Yachats River overlook, January 2011

He leaned on the rail,
ragged wool jacket pulled tight,
wild red hair tamed by a tan cap.

He turned as I approached
and gave a gap-toothed grin,
lips concealed by bushy beard.

I backpacked here, he said.
Walked most all the way.

Oh? From where?

Outside Chicago. Got tired of sittin'
in front of the TV.
Thought I'd see the Pacific
from this side.

His eyes twinkled in the sunlight.

My daughter thinks I'm crazy.
His voice cracked with laughter.
I akst 'er why she thinks
I'm on full disability.

You were in Vietnam?

He nodded. *This*, he said,
is a much better view,
and spread his arms

to embrace
the sun-sparked sea.

SYMPOSIUM

He brings me poison
words tormented love separation
a withered bouquet woven
with absinthe wormwood
abandonment boredom regret
starry anemones delicate asphodels prickly
burdock the seeming happy amethyst and canary carnations
screaming antipathy and disdain
an untranslatable orange lily
whispering hatred against a pale vase
vain dream-like clusters of hydrangeas
jealous lemon hyacinths lost
in the sorrow of their vivid violet sisters
      and
a forsaken single blood red tulip—the perfect suitor
nestled among fragrant creamy tuberoses
insinuating dangerous
lovers.

CAFÉ MORNINGS

Did I read of them first? Did their magic
rub off from novels? Or did the charm
of secondhand tables, rubbed paint trim,
green chintz half-curtains on streaky windows
capture me unaided? Simple coffee and cake days,
a pen and notebook handy, always a theme
wandering through to capture. Burly aroma
of Sumatra, Kenya; cinnamon rolls
warming in toaster ovens, the clink of change
and rustle of newspapers. Way station
of strangers, a pause in whatever lives
they were leading. Some murmured laughter,
the door opening and closing—
clunk, tinkle, clunk.
Maybe it was the quiet, the slowed pace?
Back then a café was for idling. Maybe
just my own liberty enthralled me—
like a "grown-up writer," here I was, capturing
it all on paper, sipping coffee black, dreaming
that others would envy my days.

OUT ON HER OWN

She stops me at the crosswalk
of Main & Chequessett Neck Road,
grips my hand, a regular Charles Atlas hold.

The stooped, bird-like
white-haired crone in rumpled pink
proclaims she has a story to tell.
Her stance commands onlookers
to gather, cars to slow.

I listen as she holds court—
a sovereign without a scepter,
her subjects constrained.

She relays the same account
she must have told a hundred times
to other unsuspecting souls, caught
in the lattice of her jumbled web.

The specifics of her narrative,
not interesting enough
to repeat in this small poem

but the twinge I feel
when I recognize the dire straits
of this befuddled old stranger
makes me linger,

her gnarled hand in mine
until the end of her tale.

Janice D. Rubin

VITTORIO

When I was almost nine, I rode my
ten-speed through a Portland neighborhood
past row after row of white clapboard houses
to the little mom and pop grocery store on the corner.
Leaned my luminous steed against the lamppost—
unlocked.

The u-shaped handle bars
formed like the horns of a wild ram.
A brilliant metallic blue, with the brand,
Vittorio, stamped on the frame. Vittorio
a regal lion roaring, mouth open, red tongue
surrounded by a royal Italian crest,
circled with olive branches.

Dashing out of the store
ice cream sandwich in hand
my bike was gone.

Vaporized, disappeared, it left a mark,
like a slap on the face, hot and red.
I was so proud of my birthday gift.
I patrolled the blacktop streets in SE Portland hunting
for my bike.

Renate Tilson

LILACS

Inspired by Mary Oliver's "The Bleeding-heart"

Lavender beauties
heralding spring
outline pioneer homesteads,
stone foundations, barns.
Deserted for years,
lilacs still accent the land.

I inhale the perfume
of the soft purple, an old-time favorite.
It brings crystal clear,
warm memories of mother—
her silky, delicate skin, fine, white hair.
I see her cutting lush bouquets,
arranging them in a milk pitcher
to be admired in her rustic cottage.
Such delight, simple joy, she found
adorning her beloved place with
this profuse gift of nature.

Engulfed by today's plenty
I yearn for her presence,
humility, the uncomplicated pleasures
which so enriched her life.

Now I cut lilacs,
pass lavender beauties
on to friends.

WINNOWING

i

Phil was dull, Charles too accommodating, Bill flicked crumbs on the dining room floor . . . and she wonders why I stopped introducing her to my boyfriends.

dandelions
I try to remember a time
before
mother told me
they were weeds

ii

I was elated . . . until he said *but we're leaving for the Peace Corps in two months.* Then came the long drive to Connecticut and a doctor's words that left me hollow . . . *I can fix that.*

dandelions
I close my eyes
before
blowing seeds
into the wind

iii

An aide swabs my mother's lips so deftly. He tells me I can do it but I can't. Mother hates it when I hover . . . and besides I'm remembering that time she said *why don't you have children? What did I do wrong?*

Harriot West

the meadow
stippled with dandelions
maybe
it's okay
to hug her now

COLORLINES

From the beginning, I shared classrooms and lunch tables with Mary Ortiz, Carlotta Chacón, and Julie Perez, considered them friends though they lived across an invisible line from the rest of town.

My family lived on the wrong side of a different line, one that split old from new and plenty from almost enough.

I didn't think about those lines when Ronnie whirled us to third place in that dance contest. Ronnie Ramirez: tall, handsome, best dancer in our class. I was Cinderella, he was my Prince.

It took years to understand—if his skin had matched mine, we would have won. It has taken decades to realize—if my skin had matched his, we wouldn't have had a chance.

moonless night
littered with
orange blossom stars

AMERICAN DOUGHNUT

After Marie's parents sent us home Janice headed to work. 2nd shift. I walked Rock Road to the store front, opposite direction from where I lived. Janice unlocked the heavy back door setting free a scent of powdered sugar and baked bread. I sat on a green swivel bar stool at the gold flecked Formica counter reading *The Hobbit*. Janice saved us the three fattest chocolate-dipped vanilla-cream-filled near-to-bursting doughnuts—doughnuts like helium balloons stretched to the limits. Three in case Marie made it out her bedroom window to join us. The portable Panasonic transistor radio had a long thin metal antenna and often played static. We were lucky when "Sundown," "Time in a Bottle" or "The Way We Were" blared from KSHE-95. We talked about the yearning—the losing of our virginities, if we should skip school and when, drank cup after cup of hot chocolate until her shift was over and we had to walk home alone in the dark.

COMMUNION SLIP

At seven, the thing that worried me most—
not host-choking…we'd practiced
with profane wafers, not to mention candy Neccos—
was that tulle slip under the lace and nylon skirt
of the sinless Communion dress
that cost a week's salary. That erection of a slip
sticking out like a propeller
to loft the skirt in a frozen spin
around my worried thighs.

It grated, when I tried it on,
like Mom's cheese gizmo
and I could not help wriggling
outside the dressing room
like a go-go girl under its abrasions
until Mom slapped me on the arm
and all the shoppers stared.

What if I sinned walking up the aisle,
just about to Receive—too late to confess—
would an emergency Hail Mary do the trick?

What if I tripped
and two whole rows of white-suited boys
sinned?

DESCENDANTS

After two generations you're forgotten.—Aunt Mattie

1

Our children, of course,
retain memories—loving or not.

Grandchildren might remember
the pipe smell of Dunhill London

or sugar cookie dough
rolled out on a kitchen counter.

For great-grandchildren
a framed portrait

tucked away in the linen closet
is merely that of a stranger

something to be added
to garage sale odds and ends

along with the chipped Wedgewood
no one in the family wants.

2

A great-great grandchild
rummaging in a local junk shop

might spy a familiar likeness, framed—
heart shaped face, jutting chin,

widow's peak
something about the mouth, the jaw

and on a whim
claim the old canvas

hang it beside a corner bookcase
filled with used novels bought in bulk

to make a new home ageless.

Janice D. Rubin

COUNTY CORK PUBLIC HOUSE/PORTLAND

On the wall, behind the half-filled amber bottles:
John Fitzgerald Kennedy
Edward Moore Kennedy
Pope John Paul the second,
a restoration of Vatican II and the Latin liturgy.

The penny whistle slides forth and back,
coasts over green hills,
rocky slopes of County Clare,
County Kilkenny, County Cork.

My childhood friend Sylvia plays her guitar with authority
her silver hair wild, glints like a Celtic specter.
Her musical partner Lance on a dulcimer
pounds out *Old Joe Clark* like a step dancer on a stage
or a writer drawing out a metaphor.

Pints quench a Saturday night thirst.
The barmaid with dark hair,
beauty behind black frames and thick lenses says
families with children, minors we sweep them out at 9 PM.
The working man beside me asks
how much I'll pay him to save my seat,
barstool bold, he intends to drink all night.

Through the door my sister and niece arrive
like Gaelic visions come to greet me.
We find a nook by the dart-board to listen
to the lilting tunes,
the sterling poetry of Irish history.

SUPPOSE

I outlive
my good friends,
they slip away
into the vast sea
so much younger than me

>Generous Mary Jo—shares wisdom with AFS mamas, maker
of chocolate sauces, perennial hostess.

>Fran—artist, story teller, brown curls galore, chanteuse.

>Nancy—teacher of nurses, contagious laugh, joyous sense of
humor even until the very end, the cancer.

Gone,
>their gifts of shared energy.

I am
>alone.

Suppose it was their gift to me,
>my job, to share with others
their love of life,
our connectedness,
their thoughts, energies.

And suppose
>no one wants to hear
to listen to the joy
the celebrating of memories,
my life enriched by theirs.

Renate Tilson

Nobody.

As they slip away

suppose I just let it all move on into time,
into quiet, deep, silent waters.

IN ANOTHER COUNTRY

He would never turn the furnace on until November. It seemed such a small thing, barely worth arguing over. After all I had a drawer full of woolen sweaters. So life went on. I made chili without jalapeños, listened to Coltrane instead of Tina Turner, drank Irish whisky not Pinot Noir.

If only I'd stood up for myself. But it wasn't like that. I simply moved on to the next man.

bindweed—
such an easy metaphor
he scoffs
I nod, too embarrassed
to ask what he means

SMOKING

I drift from room to room,
like wispy smoke
from one of Mom's
abandoned cigarettes.

On days like this, she'd say,
Don't waste this gorgeous day inside,
then brush away objections
and chase us out-of-doors.

Her deep New England roots
allowed her to dismiss
that in California
all year is a beautiful day.

She didn't heed her own advice,
stayed inside, smoked Pall Malls
or Tareytons and left them burning
in ashtrays black with tar.

I ached when she told
of missing treks with Dad
while she, too short of breath to join him,
waited at some trailhead . . . smoking.

Laura LeHew

A FULL ONE HUNDRED AND TWENTY COUNT BOX OF RED CRAYONS

my hand is empty my skin taut
you are a fire appearing as tongues
of light   the anatomy of a crush
you have become a terrible opposition
addition through subtraction is everything
we become terrible flames

falling angels stitched into flames
you taste like nicotine your fingers taut
are not so easily unfastened   everything
some kind of sin spoken in tongues
vows and prophecies in opposition
you have no words but everyday imply   crush

make my flesh tremble   crush
my two kinds of empty   flames
hidden beneath surface opposition
lightening when the wind curves taut
in a sky of tongues
I have been waiting for you to find me   everything

melts everything
a landscape a crush
tongues
indelible flames
imprints taut
against a rough opposition

maybe I don't want the opposition
choreographed in your August eyes   everything
feels like forever   taut

Laura LeHew

interior pieces added to the crush
rubbed raw against a stubble of flames
in a sea of something monochrome   tongues

you give me and you give me tongues
maybe there is a moment without opposition
alignment looming in flames
my heart in your hands   everything
doubts the crush
I am some other where taut

a crush of fate and we are a candle of tongues
a wick ignited through taut opposition
everything consumed in flames

LITTLE BROTHER

The D. Q.
  the Blizzard
   the dramatic upending
    his eyes in the rear view
         my backseat.

REDHEAD

When they talk of their high school days, I hear them speak of Rochelle, the classmate they all fancied—her hair, a shade that wasn't carroty, but more auburn or russet. Her long tresses cascaded in great waves, like the ocean sweeping to shore on the heels of a winter storm, drifting over the smooth pale of her cheeks as wispy strands catch the sunlight entering study hall windows.

We meet at a 50th high school reunion; her thinning silver hair is cropped short. She tells me, with retirement upon her, she has a hunger to learn Italian. We speak of rereading favorite classics. We call out Jane Austen in unison.

She asks, during a lull in our conversation, if my dark brown hair is custom blended in a salon.

crescent moon
over the mountains
crimson twilight

BLACK BEAR

The black bear wanders into town.
Spotted first in Ferguson's yard
and again at the Mitchels', by the red garden shed.
No one seems upset by his presence.
McCarty dashes into his house
finds his binoculars in the bedroom dresser drawer.

We wait, patiently taking turns with the binoculars.
I notice details of the bear's winter coat,
thick with red tones, his huge claws,
curved two inches from his toes.

We observe the bear brush up against the fence
amble across the meadow in Legacy Park
back up through the white yarrow
and blue morning glories
into the stand of Douglas firs
behind Max O'Brien's cottage.

I think of the other bears up in the hills
above the valley, less to sustain them,
few provisions from which to forage.
I know I'll see this bear again next spring.
McCarty hears his wife call over the fence
gives a shrug, turns and leaves through the gate.

I look up, overhead, wave after wave
of Canadian geese honk, fly
in an audible rippling formation,
calling to each other, anxiously.

Renate Tilson

MY BROTHER MAX

takes his life, bit by bit
isolated in his dark world, vodka, drugs—
there is no roaring suicide.

My brother's fragile soul, sensitive, and gay,
with so much promise,
contorts views, rejects—
family, love, work, creative life.

He is stressed, puzzled, confused
jobs, failed friendships, family relations,
diminishes still further today.

He is alive, taken care of, warm, fed.
Our caring, unconditionally loving parents
knew and dreaded his incorrigible reality all along,
planned and provided for him.

Parents tried their ultimate best.
Their caring never seemed right
to him, nor sufficient. Decades long we knew
he needed special attention, more love.

Did I shield him too much, or not enough?
I didn't know how to do it. My efforts all futile.

His is a half-ravaged brain—hopeless, useless.
Shrinks, docs, friends, AA all did their share.
What remains is diseased, torn apart
clinically disabled and lacking,

as good as gone.

PICKING SUNFLOWERS FOR VAN GOGH

It's not an easy task. For all his impasto and rough ways with the brush, he's extraordinarily fussy about his flowers. And he hates it when they droop. Sometimes I see him gently cup a sagging bloom. So tenderly it's easy to imagine him helping an old woman lug her panier up a rickety flight of stairs. I like him then. Despite how demanding he is to work for. Never a word of thanks. My hands stained with pollen, to say nothing of dust rags that look as though they've been steeped in saffron.

It's a pity he isn't fonder of roses. Except for those thorns. Lavender perhaps? I'd fancy that. Brushing my fingertips along the stalks, carrying their scent throughout the day, dreaming about a wild man with ginger hair and reckless ways.

heat wave
the honey bee's
restless thrum

ACKNOWLEDGMENTS

Thanks to the editors of the following journals and books in which these poems first appeared, sometimes in altered versions or with different titles:

Darling, Lee. "Colorlines." *Haibun Today*, 11:2, June, 2017.

LeHew, Laura. "A Full One Hundred Count Box of Red Crayons." *Homestead Review*, 2007.

LeHew, Laura. "Symposium." *Her Mark Calendar 2009*, Woman Made Gallery, 2009.

McGuire, Catherine. "Communion Slip." *Eunoia*, 2016.

Munson, Sharon Lask. "Descendants." *Popshot*, 2015.

West, Harriot. "In Another Country." *KYSO Flash 4*, Fall, 2015. 2nd place winner, "Best of Haibun and Tanka Forms" contest.

West, Harriot. "Picking Flowers for Van Gogh." *KYSO Flash 6*, Fall, 2016. *Best Small Fictions 2017*, Braddock Avenue Books.

West, Harriot. "Winnowing." *Haibun Today*, 11:1, March 2017.

BIOGRAPHIES

After she retired from a career in computer programming, **Lee Darling** transformed her love of logic and language and began building poems and other written works: a novel, *(Just Out of Reach,* 2011*)*, a book of traditional haiku, *(Sundrops,* 2016*)*, many personal essays and letters to the editor.

See her blog at scatteredbumps.blogspot.com.

(Rebecca) Lee Darling was born in Boston, raised in the L.A. basin and escaped to Eugene, Oregon in 1961 at age 18. She is a "Double Duck," with two degrees from the University of Oregon. Her graduate work analyzing sociological data provided the path to a career in computers.

Laura lives in the realm of possibility, where anything can happen. She is constantly thinking of new ideas and themes to convey in her work. Her intent is to create works that are formally and aesthetically engaging while conceptually connecting with the everyday; to reify the ordinary into the extraordinary; to question realities—social, political and otherwise. Poetry is a way to explore and understand those ideas which frustrate and confront her.

Widely published **Laura LeHew**'s collections include: *Becoming* (Another New Calligraphy) a non-linear discourse on alcoholism and dementia, *Willingly Would I Burn*, (MoonPath Press) themed around math and science, *It's Always Night, It Always Rains*, (Winterhawk Press) noir and *Beauty* (Tiger's Eye Press) fairy tales. Laura received her MFA from CCA. She owns and edits Uttered Chaos, a small press which publishes books of poetry by NW writers. Laura knows nothing of gardens or gardening but is well versed in the cultivation of cats.

utteredchaos.org ● lauralehew.com

Catherine McGuire is a writer and artist with a deep concern for our planet's future. She has three decades of published poetry, four poetry chapbooks and a full-length poetry book, *Elegy for the 21ˢᵗ Century* (FutureCycle Press). Her fiction includes a number of science fiction short stories and a de-industrial science fiction novel, *Lifeline* (Founders House Publishing). Find her at www.cathymcguire.com.

Different things motivate me to write. A mood. A memory. The smell of cooking. Burning leaves. A windy day. Rain. Fog. Music. Someone or something I observe or overhear—and, of course, imagination. I have a pin that says, "I Make Things Up." It's important for me to have my own office. I took over a spare bedroom, emptied it of bed and dresser and moved in the essentials: a desk for my computer, a bookshelf, a file cabinet, and an old cushioned chair of my mother's that goes back to my childhood. From my upstairs office window, I look out on tall oaks. The trees and the changing seasons add a kind of peace that makes writing possible.

Sharon Lask Munson was born and raised in Detroit, Michigan. She taught in England, Germany, Okinawa and Puerto Rico before driving to Anchorage, Alaska and staying put for the next twenty years. She is a poet, retired teacher, coffee addict, wine lover, old movie enthusiast—with many published poems, two chapbooks, and one full length book of poetry. She now lives and writes in Eugene, Oregon.

Janice D. Rubin

My writing process starts with a visual impression, an experience or a memory. I may observe something or read something that sparks an idea for a piece. My poems evolve in images, colors, emotions and language. I'm a diligent observer of the small details of life. Elizabeth Bishop wrote "Catch a peripheral vision of whatever it is one can never really see full-face but that seems enormously important." The discipline of the weekly Monday writing group, bringing a poem each week is very helpful. Even with rewriting and revision I try to maintain the original spark, the inspiration for the poem. As a counselor I do lots of report writing, but my creative writing always re-energizes me.

Janice D. Rubin is a counselor and educator. She received her M.S. from the University of Oregon and her B.A. in English Literature. Her poems have been published in the *Austin International Poetry Festival Anthology*, *Tiger's Eye Poetry Journal*, *Glass: A Journal of Poetry*, *Arabesque Journal*, *The Quizzical Chair Anthology* and other journals. She was nominated for the Pushcart Poetry Prize in 2008. She's taught at Oregon State University and currently teaches at Lane Community College. She's the author of *Transcending Damnation Creek Trail & Other Poems* (Flutter Press 2010). Her full-length collection *Tin Coyote* is forthcoming (Blue Light Press, 2018).

Renate Tilson, a former teacher, is tri-lingual, the mother of three and now grandmother of five grandchildren. A born New Englander who maintains strong ties there, she is a graduate of the University of Vermont. Renate is a Master Gardener and has been on public radio commenting on gardening for 12 years, and is regularly published in Oregon lifestyle magazines.

Harriot West lives in Eugene, Oregon. Her first book, *Into the Light,* a collection of haibun (Mountains and Rivers Press, 2014), tied for first place in the Haiku Society of America's Kanterman Book Awards. Her work appears in journals and anthologies, including *Modern Haiku, Frogpond, Contemporary Haibun Online, The Norton Anthology of Haiku in English* and *The Best Small Fictions 2017.* She is a three-time winner of the *Modern Haiku* award for favorite haibun as well as a recipient of the Museum of Haiku Literature Award. She has recently completed her second manuscript, *Shades of Absence* and is working on her third, a collection of ekphrastic poems.

mountainsandriverspress.org

ABOUT RHETORICAL DEVICES

Poetry is eternal graffiti written in the heart of everyone. ~Lawrence Ferlinghetti

The day after graduating with my MFA in Poetry from the California College of Arts I decided to move from San Francisco to Eugene, Oregon. I had just joined Kim Addonizio's private critique group. It was fabulous. I didn't want to give it up. The only people I knew in Eugene were my now ex-husband and the contractors working on the house. Kim suggested I contact Dorianne Laux. Dorianne and Joe were just moving to North Carolina and suggested I contact the Lane Literary Guild.

The Guild pointed me to Gary Adams who had room in his group *P3*. I was in that group for a while when Robin Saxton was asked to form the next group for the Guild. She did and I moved into her group. *P4* otherwise known as *Poetry4*. And then, I took it over. Eventually. There was no coup. She was spending more time painting. It was a natural transition. Somewhere in there I became a member of the Guild's steering committee, where I remain to this day.

I changed the name from *P4* to the *Let Them Eat Cake Poets*. We had cakes at every birthday. There were, it seemed, a lot of birthdays. After enough turnover and after we gave up cake the group eventually re-named itself the *Rhetorical Devices*, the RDs for short.

We have had a lot of successes: poems published, books published, nominations and awards. We owe it all to the commitment of each of our members to honor and respect all the individual members, to showing up week after week, doing the work (writing, reading, going to readings, etc.) and by encouraging our members to write in their own voices. It has been a pleasure to facilitate this amazing group.

Laura LeHew

www.ingramcontent.com/pod-product-compliance
Lightning Source LLC
Chambersburg PA
CBHW072040060426
42449CB00010BA/2367